Eric Liddell: Born to Run

Also in the Blackbird Series

Blackbird Biographies

21118523N   TS

~k is i

Eric Liddell:
Born to Run

Peter Watkins

Illustrated by Gavin Rowe

Julia MacRae Books
A division of Franklin Watts

For Becky Lane

Text © 1983 Peter Watkins
Illustrations © 1983 Gavin Rowe
All rights reserved
First published in Great Britain 1983 by
Julia MacRae Books
A division of Franklin Watts Ltd.
12a Golden Square, London W1R 4BA
and Franklin Watts Inc.
387 Park Avenue South, New York 10016.

British Library Cataloguing in Publication Data
Watkins, Peter
    Eric Liddell: Born to Run.—(Blackbird series)
    1. Liddell, Eric 2. Missionaries—
    China—Biography—Juvenile literature
    3. Missionaries—Scotland—Biography—
    Juvenile literature
    I. Title   II. Series
    266'.0092'4   BV3427.L5/
    ISBN 0–86203–129–X UK edition
    ISBN 0–531–03755–X US edition
    Library of Congress Catalog Card No: 83–60634

Phototypeset by Ace Filmsetting Ltd, Frome, Somerset
Made and printed in Great Britain by Camelot Press, Southampton

Chapter 1

Eric Liddell was born in January, 1902, at a mission house in Tientsin in China. His parents were hiding there because the lives of all Christian missionaries like themselves were in great danger from the Boxers.

The Boxer Rebellion had started

in China in June, 1900. The aim of
the Boxers, who were very violent
people, was to do away with
Christian foreigners. The trouble
had arisen through the bad
behaviour of many countries
including Britain, France, Germany
and Russia, who had pushed their
way into China and demanded

property to use as trading posts. People from these countries often did not consider the feelings of Chinese people. For instance, outside one park used by Europeans only, was a notice: 'No Dogs or Chinese Allowed to Enter'. Although some of the Christian missionaries did not behave as badly as this, they

did not always fully understand the old Chinese religious customs and way of life. There were, of course, cruel and bad things about Chinese life: girls from the age of five, for example, had their feet bound to keep them small because women with big feet were looked down on.

It was essential for the missionaries to respect Chinese

traditions if they were to do their work properly. Many of the missionaries were educated people, humble and courageous, who were sympathetic towards the people and their history. James and Mary Liddell, Eric's parents, were among these. They had come from Scotland, and it was nine years before they returned there with Eric, aged six, and his elder brother, Rob.

Before their parents went back to China the two boys were sent to school at Eltham College. There the brothers' love of sports became evident. In 1918 they were first and second in the long and high jumps, the 100 yards, the hurdle race, the quarter mile and the cross country run. Eric was also captain of both the school cricket and rugby teams before he went to Edinburgh University to study science.

In his first year at Edinburgh he entered the University Sports, winning the 100 yards and coming second in the 220—the only time that he ever lost a race in Scotland. Eric was well on the way to proving himself an extraordinary athlete. His achievements were particularly surprising since a childhood illness in China had once left him so weak in the legs that someone had remarked, "That boy will never be able to run again!"

Eric Liddell was awarded the prize for being the best athlete in the Scottish Championships in 1923, 1924 and 1925. In July 1923 he competed in the Amateur Athletic Association Championships in London, where his performance made him famous throughout Great Britain. He won not only the 220 yards but also the 100 yards, creating a new British record of 9.7 seconds. This record was not beaten for thirty-five years.

In the following week, he ran one of the greatest races in the history of athletics during the three-cornered match between England, Scotland and Ireland. After winning the 100 yards and the 220, he was knocked off the track by another competitor at the start of the 440. When he got to his feet he was 20 yards behind the rest of the field. He then did the impossible: he chased them, closed the gap and went on to win with two yards to spare.

His achievement meant that he certainly would be chosen to represent Great Britain in the following year at the 1924 Olympic Games in Paris.

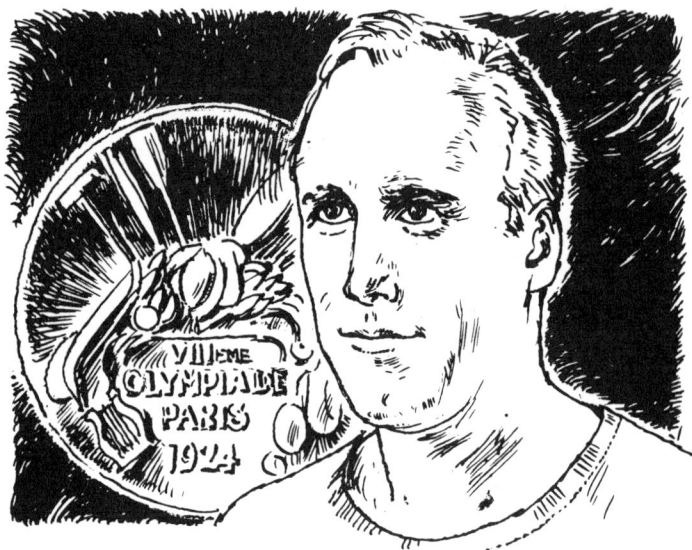

Chapter 2

Athletics was only one of the sports
that Eric excelled at whilst at
Edinburgh. During his second year
at university he was chosen to play
in two rugby trial matches in
Scotland when the best players are
selected for the national team.

Eric was selected, and Scotland only lost once in the seven internationals in which he played for them. One of the victories was against Wales at Cardiff Arms Park in 1923. This was the first time that Scotland had won there for thirty-three years! Because of his speed and skill on the rugby field, Eric was known as 'The Flying Scotsman'. However, as the Olympic Games approached Eric had to concentrate on his athletics.

British athletics in the 1920's was a much more modest affair than it is today. Runners like Eric Liddell did not receive generous money allowances nor were athletics meetings sponsored by well-known companies. Today money seems to matter much more in athletics than it did then. Conditions for the runners, too, were quite different because they didn't have special lightweight clothing and shoes, and the running tracks were often bumpy grass fields or cinder tracks. Today these tracks are carefully designed: they have smooth curves and synthetic resin 'Tartan' surfaces. Eric ran in long shorts and he used a trowel to dig small holes in the track in which he placed his feet at the start of a race. Nowadays special starting blocks are used.

Eric was only 5 feet 9 inches tall,

which is not very tall for a sprinter. When he ran his arms rotated like windmills in the air; and he would throw his head so far back that spectators wondered whether he could actually see where he was going. Eric's sprinting action was inefficient, but he raced with wild delight. Some men praise God by speaking or singing. Eric praised God by the enthusiasm of his running.

The British public was looking forward to Eric Liddell competing in the 100 metres at this eighth Olympic Games for he seemed certain to come home with a medal. In the Olympic Games races are measured in metres and kilometres rather than yards and miles as they then were in Great Britain. When Eric flatly refused to run in the heats for this race, and for the relay events, the British public and the athletic authorities were dismayed. But they were not surprised. These heats were scheduled to be run on a Sunday, and Eric Liddell firmly believed that Sunday should be kept as the Lord's

Day for Christian worship. He was not going to alter his beliefs or the pattern by which he had led his life for the chance of winning a medal.

In the end it was found possible to enter him for two longer races, the 200 metres and the 400.

The Olympic Games opened on Saturday, 5 July 1924, in the Colombes Stadium in Paris. Forty-four nations took part. The Americans came with an impressive party of four hundred athletes and their team was supported by trainers and masseurs and even a chaplain. The British team was encouraged by the presence of Edward, Prince of Wales.

On Sunday, Eric Liddell went to preach at a Scottish church in Paris, when he could have been competing in the heats of the 100 metres. On Monday, Harold Abrahams of Great Britain won the semi-final and final of that race. On Tuesday, Douglas Lowe, also of Great Britain, won the 800 metres final. On Wednesday, Liddell was third in the 200 metres final. The British athletes were obviously in fine heart and form.

Eric got into the final of the 400 metres on Friday. He had bad luck in the draw and had to run in the outside lane. From that position it was impossible for him to see how

near to or far from his rivals he was.
He set off at a staggering pace,
covering the first 200 metres in only
a slightly slower time than that of
the winner of the 200 metres. No one
thought that he could keep going.
He had set off too quickly, people
were thinking. But back went Eric's
head, and forward went his chin,

and amazingly, he surged even further ahead.

The Edinburgh *Evening News* reported, "People were on their feet cheering madly, and as if by magic, hosts of Union Jacks appeared above the heads of the raving crowd as Liddell ripped through the tape and into the arms of the Britishers who were waiting for him. For a moment the cheering lasted, then from the loudspeaker came: 'Hello, hello. Winner of the 400 metres: Liddell of Great Britain. The time 47.6 seconds is a new world record'."

Eric Liddell received a hero's welcome when he returned to Edinburgh for his graduation. He

had passed his exams and he was
presented with the degree of
Bachelor of Science. He was carried
in a sedan-chair by the students
through the streets, and was then
crowned, like the ancient Greek
Olympic victors, with an olive
wreath. "Mr Liddell," the Vice-
Chancellor of the university said to
him, "you have shown that none can
pass you but the examiner."

Chapter 3

With his university degree and with his fame as a sportsman there would have been many opportunities for Eric Liddell to follow a successful career in Great Britain. Instead, however, Eric had decided to follow the example of his parents and older brother, to serve the people of China as a missionary.

Before he went out to China he had to spend a year at the Scottish Congregational College in Edinburgh, preparing himself for conditions abroad and adding to his knowledge of the country. He also had to learn more about the Christian faith.

When he left Scotland he was drawn to Waverley Station by Edinburgh students in a carriage decorated with ribbons and streamers. Huge crowds on the platforms sang hymns until his train was out of sight.

Eric was returning to the very

place in which he had been born, to Tientsin, a large and sprawling industrial and trading town. The unsettled China that he had left almost twenty years ago as a small boy was still full of disturbances. Much of the land was under the control of the war-lords, who did not bother about law and order or peace and prosperity. They went their own

way, continually fighting each other with their private armies, destroying harvests and kidnapping women and children. And all the time the poor peasants suffered from the additional disasters of floods and famines.

In big cities like Tientsin, where there were international trading centres and representatives from foreign countries, there was less chaos, although there were still demonstrations, protests and strikes.

Eric became a teacher at the Tientsin Anglo-Chinese College, probably the finest British School in North China. Among his duties there were those of sports master and science teacher. He had to work very hard as he was not naturally good at everything he did. He was frequently invited to talk about Christianity and although not a gifted speaker, people listened intently to what he had to say. He did not try to say clever things but linked the words of Jesus with his own experience of life to show why he wanted to live a Christian life.

Everyone was attracted by Eric Liddell's charm and sincerity, but his popularity never made him big-headed just as his athletic fame had never gone to his head.

Eric did not give up competitive running and rugby playing when he became a missionary teacher. In China he was still capable of producing world-class performances. When the Amsterdam Olympics came round in 1928 he was only twenty-six years old. It is possible that, having been the world's greatest quarter-miler, he could have become the world's greatest half-miler.

In 1928, although he did not compete in Europe in the Olympic Games, he created another Liddell legend in the East at an international athletics meeting. He won the 400 metres, but he only had half an hour after the race to catch the boat home. He rushed straight

from the finishing tape to a taxi, but
he was twice stopped in his tracks
when national anthems were played,
during which he stood to attention.
The boat was already moving out
when he arrived at the quayside, but
he threw his bags on it and, like a
gazelle, made an immense jump
after them!

26

Chapter 4

Eric returned to Scotland for a
year between 1931 and 1932 for
furlough or holiday. 'Furlough' is
the word used to describe the time
that missionaries spend in their
home country. It is often a very busy
time, when they are asked to give
talks about their work abroad. It

28

was by no means a complete year of rest for Eric. He completed a course of study at the Scottish Congregational College, and was ordained minister or pastor: he became the Reverend Eric Liddell. He was invited to speak all over Scotland before making his way back to China.

Coming from and returning to Tientsin he travelled via Canada, where he visited a girl called Florence McKenzie. Her parents were Canadian missionaries in China, and Eric had known her for a long while. They had become engaged in 1930, but delayed getting married until she had qualified as a

trained nurse in Toronto. They were prepared to wait patiently for their marriage in the good cause of the missionary work. Their wedding eventually took place in Tientsin on 27 March 1934.

Eric and Florence had two

daughters and enjoyed a happy family life. Eric was a proud father. Then in 1937 came another of those separations for the sake of Eric's important work in another part. Eric was sent to join his brother, Rob, in the Siaochang area, where he had spent the first five years of his life with his parents.

Eric visited his wife and family whenever he could, but the journey from Siaochang to Tientsin was always dangerous. The Japanese had invaded that part of China and as well as fighting against the Japanese invaders there was also civil war, which caused much misery for everyone. Pastor Liddell—he was

called 'Li Mu Shi' in Chinese—
taught the hospital staff to care for
each soldier as a child of God.

On one occasion he set out to
rescue a wounded man who had
been left to die in a temple. No one
else bothered about the man.
Japanese soldiers had made him
kneel down, and an officer had
savagely slashed his sword down on

him. The man dropped to the ground with a ghastly gash on his neck. He was left for dead. Eric managed to get him to the hospital where he eventually recovered.

In 1939, at the approach of the

Second World War, the Liddell family were reunited and returned again to Scotland, via Canada. On their way back to China their ship was hit by a German torpedo, but it failed to explode. By the end of October, 1940, Eric's family was settled in Tientsin once more, and he had returned to Siaochang. But the situation had got even worse while he had been away.

Early in 1941 the Japanese authorities ordered all the missionaries to leave the Siaochang area. This meant that Eric was able to be with his family in Tientsin. Nevertheless, even that town was no longer safe for his wife and children, and so, in May, 1941, Florence and their two much loved daughters left for Canada. Four months later Eric was informed by telegram that he was the father of a third girl, Maureen—a child he was never to see.

In March, 1943, with hundreds of other British and Americans, he was moved on Japanese orders to a camp at Weihsien. 1,800 people, of all ages and from all walks of life were crammed together in a small area. There were no decent living quarters and sanitation. They had to do the best they could to get on with each other, which often was not very well.

Eric, however, had the wonderful
talent of getting on with everyone.
His good humour prevented bad-
tempered squabbles and conflicts
from growing. He saw that the
teenagers were bored and he
immediately set about teaching them
what they should have been learning

at school. He organised games, plays, craft and puppet shows— every possible activity and entertainment.

The young people were fired by his enthusiasm, and made happier by his boyish sense of fun. He mended their hockey sticks and

baseballs. He did odd jobs for those who were too weak to help themselves. He went out of his way to make friends with people who were despised by others in the camp. Nothing was too much trouble for him. His life, one woman there wrote, "was grounded in God, in faith, and in trust".

But it was certainly no holiday camp. Food and medicine were in short supply and the strain of living in such unhealthy conditions resulted in much physical and mental sickness. There were many deaths from typhoid and malaria, acute malnutrition and dysentery.

Eric himself began to grow weak.

He had been burning up his energy
in helping the other prisoners, but
now there were times when he was
completely exhausted and depressed.
He had never burdened others with
his troubles, but he could not hide
the fact that he was having painful
headaches. His right leg was partly
paralysed, and he even had difficulty
in speaking clearly. No one really
knew what was the matter with him.
In a final fit of coughing and

vomiting, he muttered to the nurse beside him, "It's complete surrender." He had always wanted his life to be ordered by God. Was he then, in the last moments of his life, completely surrendering himself to the will of God?

On the day after he died in January, 1945, it was discovered that he had had a tumour on the left side of his brain. Even with the proper medical equipment it would

have been impossible to operate successfully.

Everyone in Scotland mourned when the news of his death was announced. He had been their greatest and best-loved athlete. In Glasgow the *Evening News* reported: "Scotland has lost a son who did her proud every hour of his life."

Although Eric Liddell was an extremely tough and determined man he was also a brave and modest one. He was always able to cheer people up, to make them feel confident and good because he made them feel loved.

His quiet strength of character was built up each morning with a private and silent hour of meditation and Bible study. This helped him, no doubt, to put the most important things first in his life: loving and serving God and his fellow men.

The story of Eric Liddell is not only about a famous sportsman; it is also about a kind of Christian saint.